THE
HIDING
GAME

THE HIDING GAME

GWEN STRAUSS

illustration by

Herb Leonhard

PELICAN PUBLISHING COMPANY

GRETNA 2017

OCTOBER 1940

All summer, Aube's family moved from place to place, staying one step ahead of the German soldiers. When Aube asked if they would return home to Paris, Papa looked worried and Mama looked sad. Then one day, a man named Danny made their worried faces disappear. He led them down the long, shaded driveway to a special place.

Papa explained that there was a magician named Varian Fry, and Danny Bénédite was his assistant. They helped people hide and escape. Danny had found the Villa Air-Bel, the enchanted place where they would live together until it was their turn to flee to safety.

Aube liked Sundays, because Papa and Mama's friends gathered at the Villa Air-Bel to play games. Like her parents, the friends who came on Sunday were also thinkers, artists and writers who had to hide from the German soldiers because of their ideas of freedom and liberty. They played charades. They danced to music from the radio. Papa set out sheets of paper, pots of glue, colored pencils, newspapers and scissors on the long table, and everyone made collages together. Sometimes they played Aube's favorite game: *Cadavre Exquis*. A piece of paper was folded like a fan, and each person drew a part on one fold without seeing the drawings of the others. When they

unfolded the paper, wonderful and silly mixed-up creatures emerged.

Papa said that "by singing, playing and laughing with the greatest joy," they would fight against fear.

Varian loved birds, and he taught Aube how to look through binoculars at the birds flying freely in their garden. One night he found a bird that had flown into the glass window. The bird was not dead, only stunned, he said.

Danny carefully carried the bird inside, where everyone looked on. There was Danny, his wife Theo and son Peterkin, Varian and his dog Clovis, and Victor Serge and his son Vlady.

In Danny's hands, the bird slowly woke up.
Then Danny carefully took the bird to the window.
Everyone cheered as the bird flew safely out into
the tall tree branches.

There were many hidden things in the Villa. They kept the radio hidden. They kept a cow hidden in the yard for milk. Mama explained that if the authorities found out, they would take away the cow because food was scarce. The cook was often frustrated because there was no sugar, very little bread, and only pretend coffee made by roasting acorns. When there was no meat for dinner, Papa placed a drawing of a roast beef in the kitchen pantry to make the cook laugh.

Varian and Danny knew the authorities were reading their mail and listening to their phone calls. They found a way to send a secret message: they rolled a long piece of paper into the finger of a plastic glove, tied it, and hid it in a tooth-paste tube. This way, they were able to slip messages past the border guards about who they would be sneaking out next and when.

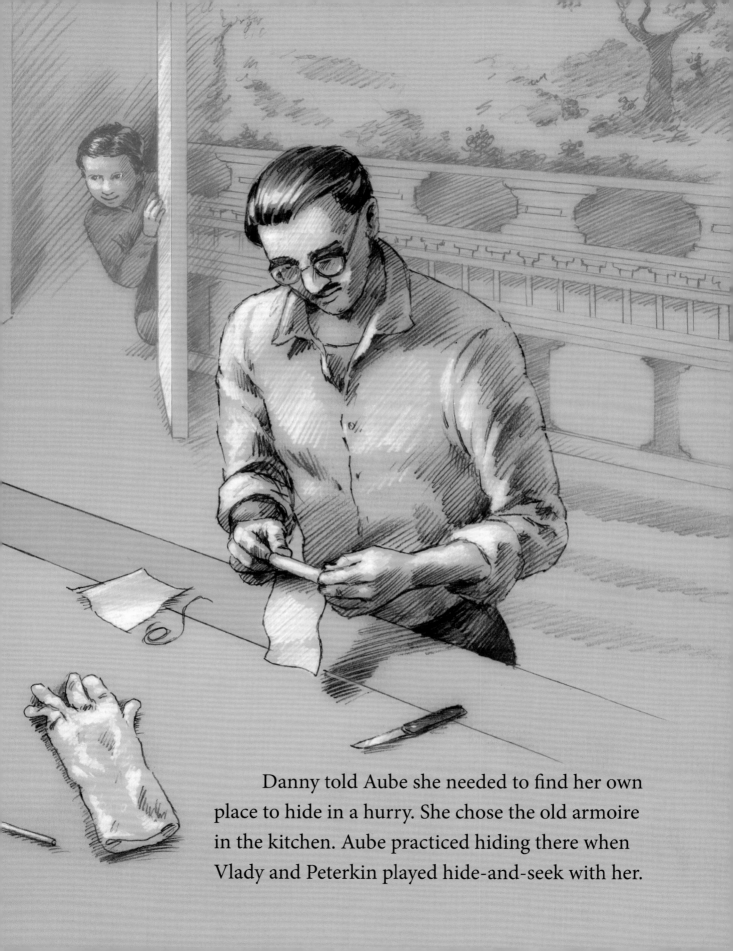

Danny told Aube she needed to find her own place to hide in a hurry. She chose the old armoire in the kitchen. Aube practiced hiding there when Vlady and Peterkin played hide-and-seek with her.

When a group was about to make the
dangerous journey to a new country, they
held a Sunday party and art sale to raise
money. Danny climbed high into the giant
tree and hung paintings from the branches.
Aube loved Monsieur Chagall's angels best.
She felt his angels were protecting them.

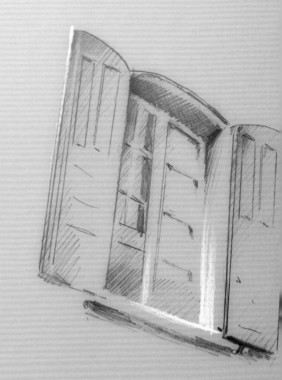

As winter approached, Danny and Varian prepared another group to escape. They would take a train to the border, where Danny arranged for a guide to lead them over the mountains. The guide had half a scrap of torn paper. Danny gave the group leader the other half, like a matching puzzle piece. They would show it to their guide and if the two halves matched, the guide would know Danny had sent them.

Aube heard Varian tell them to wait for the green light.

This warning reminded Aube of a game she played with Vlady and Papa, called "red light, green light," where the leader controlled the players' actions by calling green light— allowing them to run—and red light—telling them to freeze in place. If you moved at the wrong moment, you lost.

The cold weather slipped through the windows and under the door-frames of the villa. They had to wear all their clothes at once to keep warm. Vlady was too busy with the other men gathering firewood to play with Aube. Peterkin had been sent to his grandmother's, where there was more food to eat. Aube had no one to play with.

At night they gathered in one room and listened to the news of the war on the radio. After the news, Danny would start to sing a French tune. Each person would choose their own song to sing.

Varian liked a funny American song about a pony. Victor and his son Vlady sang a Russian song, sounding like soldiers marching. Everyone clapped when it was Aube's turn.

Danny went away for a week, and when he returned he was upset about the camps he had visited. They were terrible places where the authorities put people. Aube understood now that the danger was that they would be sent to the camps. Danny was writing a letter to protest the conditions.

In those camps, people were dying of disease and
starvation. They had no blankets and barely enough
clothes. It was snowing now. Danny said that all those
people were going to freeze.

Aube stood there thinking of the game of freeze tag.
If you were tagged, you had to stand still until someone
on your side released you. She thought of all those
people freezing, waiting for someone to set them free.

One wintry afternoon, in early December, Aube heard car wheels on the gravel and then Danny's wife screaming, "Police!"

Men in uniform burst into the villa. Papa quickly threw some papers into the fire. Mama grabbed Aube's hand and gave her a squeeze. Aube started to cry. The police were yelling at Varian and Papa. They had to inspect every room.

"Unbelieveable!" Papa shouted as the police led him up to their rooms. The police found collages that had been made during the Sunday games and said these were dangerous crimes. They had to take everyone with them, but after Danny and Varian talked to them, they agreed to leave the women and children behind at the Villa.

Aube didn't want to see them take away her Papa. She ran to the armoire and crouched down, hidden inside with Clovis curled next to her.

As she sat there holding Clovis tightly, she wondered if they would take Papa and the others to the camps. Would their coats keep them warm?

Mama found her and told her the men would be gone for only a few hours.

But hours became days.

The villa was silent—no songs, no laughter, no Sunday games.

In the dark she whispered, "Green light, green light, green light."

A week later, the men were released. But Papa said it wouldn't be long until the police came back, and the next time they wouldn't be so lucky.

Danny and Varian went to work preparing their escape. But before they left, Papa gathered all the artists together for one last game: they would create a collective artwork from a deck of playing cards. The cards would remind them that they had laughed together and stayed free in their hearts even during the darkest times. Aube watched as each artist picked a card from Papa's hat. The artists would then create their own version of the card they had picked.

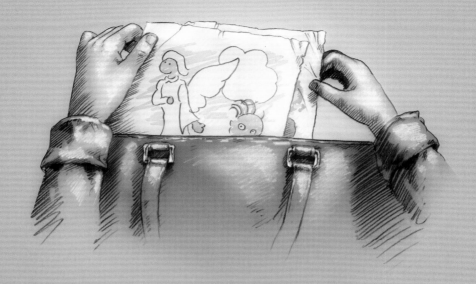

At last, Varian and Danny found a way to
get Serge's family and Aube's family passage
on a ship to South America. They would all
leave together. And on February 18, 1941, Aube
waved goodbye to Clovis, Varian, and Danny.

The journey took longer than a month.

At sea, Aube looked at the few things she
was able to bring and remembered how the
artist Marcel Duchamp once visited the Villa
with a small suitcase. When he opened it, there
was a collection of all his favorite artworks, like
a miniature museum.

Aube had her own museum in a bag—her
collection of drawings from the villa.

Several months after Aube's departure, Varian was forced to leave France and return to America. Danny left the villa and went underground so he could continue hiding people in small villages and forests around the region. He helped another 300 people escape France. Then in 1943, Danny's magic seemed to run out. He was arrested by the Nazis and sentenced to death.

But then, just as he was being led to the prison courtyard to face the firing squad, soldiers fighting against the Nazis arrived at the gates to free the inmates. The guards lowered their rifles and surrendered, and Danny lived to tell his story.

The History

Danny Bénédite was my great-uncle.

Varian Fry first arrived in Marseille, France, in 1940, soon after the start of World War II in Europe. The Nazis had defeated France and the north part of the country was invaded by Germany. Thousands of people fled south. Marseille was full of refugees, artists, anti-Nazi writers, philosophers, musicians, and Jews, all in danger of being sent to the death camps. Varian had come from America with a list of 200 names and $3,000 taped to his leg. A group in New York called the American Rescue Committee had sent him. He was supposed to stay for one month and get the people on his list out of France. But seeing how desperate the

refugees were, Varian soon realized he could not save just 200. He had to save as many lives as possible, and he would stay in France until he was forced out.

To save lives, Varian created two groups, one that was legal and one that was secret, and he hired a group of courageous people to work with him. The American Relief Center was a legal group openly helping the refugees by giving them food and money. The other secret group found many ways to hide and smuggle those who were most in danger out of France. Because the work was hard and dangerous, they needed a place to rest outside of Marseille, away from the police who were always

At left, Daniel Bénédite and Varian Fry, 1940

Above, Aube Breton with her father, André Breton

Aube's Mother, Jacqueline Lamba

Aube and her family escape aboard the converted cargo ship Capitane Paul-LeMerle.

At left, Theo, Peterkin, and Danny on a picnic, c. 1940

Above, the Villa Air-Bel, where Aube and her family lived in 1940-41.

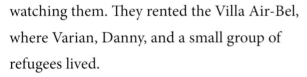

Above, Aube with her mother and father eating breakfast at the Villa Air-Bel, 1940.

Above right, Sylvain Itkine, Jacques Herold, Aube, and her father gathering wood, 1941.

watching them. They rented the Villa Air-Bel, where Varian, Danny, and a small group of refugees lived.

Because of the efforts of Varian, Danny, and the Rescue Committee, 2,200 people got out of Nazi-controlled France. And for the people they could not get out, it is estimated that their efforts saved over 4,000 more lives, by keeping families hidden and fed during the war. Among the people they saved were some of the most important scientists, artists, writers, and thinkers of the time.

Those who were saved were always grateful. But for a long time the French and American governments did not recognize the Rescue Committee's achievements. Few people knew

about Varian Fry. In 1967, twenty-six years later, because of the insistence of some of the artists they had saved, the French government recognized Varian and Danny by awarding them the Legion d'Honneur. Varian died six months later.

In 1991, 50 years after his courageous actions in France and 24 years after his death, Varian received his first recognition from the United States. The Holocaust Memorial Council awarded him the Eisenhower Liberation Medal. Then, in 1995, Varian Fry became the first United States citizen to be listed in the "Righteous Among the Nations" at Israel's national Holocaust Memorial, Yad Vashem. He was awarded the additional honor of

Jacques Herold helps Danny Bénédite (in the tree) hang the exhibition of Max Ernst in 1940.

Above, Aube's mother, Jacqueline, hangs upside down on a swing at the Villa Air-Bel.

"Commemorative Citizenship of the State of Israel" on January 1st, 1998. The square in front of the American Consulate in Marseille was renamed Place Varian Fry. A street in Berlin was named Varian-Fry-Straße. In 2005, a street in his hometown of Ridgewood, New Jersey, was renamed Varian Fry Way. Today, Varian Fry is known as the American Schindler.

Guests of the Villa

Gathered at the Villa were an extraordinary group of artists and writers.

Aube's father was the famous poet **André Breton**. He is known as the Pope of Surrealism. The game *Cadavre Exquis* (pronounced Kah-dah-vra X-kees) was invented by him. Aube's mother was Jacqueline Lamba, a surrealist painter.

Vlady and **Victor Serge**. Victor was a Russian revolutionary and a writer who fought against racism and anti-Semitism. He spent most of his life fleeing from fascism. But he never stopped writing. He wrote seven novels, a book of poems and six works of history. He and Vlady eventually made it safely to Mexico. Vlady Serge became one of Mexico's leading painters and muralists.

Max Ernst was a German painter, sculptor, graphic artist, and poet. He spoke out against the Nazis and moved to France. But when the war broke out he was first arrested under suspicion of being a German spy, and then later arrested for being anti- Hitler. The second time he was sent to the Camps des Milles near Aix-en-Provence. With the help of the Rescue Committee, he was released.

   After he made it safely to New York City, Ernst helped inspire the development of Abstract Expressionism.

Marc Chagall was Jewish, but because he was so famous, he did not fully understand the danger posed by the German victory in France. He was arrested by the Gestapo and was only saved because Varian Fry called the police station and warned them they were going to cause an international scandal by arresting the most famous artist in the world. A frightened policeman released him to Varian, who quickly smuggled Chagall and his wife Bella out of the country.

Marcel Duchamp was a French artist who is considered by some to be one of the most important artists of the 20th century. Duchamp challenged how people thought about art through subversive actions such as dubbing a urinal "art" and naming it "Fountain." In many ways he was the first conceptual performance artist. The suitcase he shows Aube was called *boite-en-valise*, or "box in a suitcase."

Many other important artists and writers who visited the Villa for the Sunday games were saved by the Rescue Committee but were not named in this story. Among them were Hannah Arendt, Jean Arp, Wilhelm Herzog, Wilfredo Lam, Wanda Landowska, Jacques Lipchitz, Alma Mahler Gropius Werfel, Heinrich Mann, André Masson, Otto Meyerhof, and Benjamin Péret.

Endnotes

Pp. 6-7 André Breton believed that surrealism and art must keep the playful child inside us alive. He believed that laughter was fundamentally the opposite of fascism. This quote comes from Rosemary Sullivan's book, *Villa Air-Bel*.

Pp. 8-9 Victor and Danny were old friends from Paris. Victor was the first person Danny invited to come stay at the Villa. Victor then asked Danny to invite Aube's family. This quote is from Danny's book, *La Filiere Marseillaise, Un Chemin vers las liberté sous l'occupation*.

Pp. 20-21 As part of the Rescue Committee's legal activities, Danny visited all the camps in the area and lodged complaints about the bad conditions. He fought to get people released, and he wrote a lengthy report of protest. Varian took this report to the Vichy government and to the US embassy, but no one cared. Both Varian Fry in his book *Assignment: Rescue, An Autobiography* and Danny in his book, *La Filiere Marseillaise*, wrote about their efforts to improve conditions in the camps.

Pp. 22-23 In his book, *La Filiere Marseillaise*, Danny describes what happened when the police arrived at the villa on Monday, December 3, 1940. The president of the Vichy government, Marechal Petain was visiting Marseille. To be sure that nothing happened during his visit, the authorities arrested thousands of "suspicious" people throughout Marseille.

They put them on ships in the harbor in temporary prisons. Once the visit was over, most of the people were released. But this event gave the occupants of the Villa a scare and they realized their time was running out.

Pp. 26-27 Breton thought that artists working together collectively should explore the subconscious. With this in mind, he came up with the idea of making a new deck of playing cards, which would become famous as the Jeu de Marseille. They took a regular deck and changed the four suits. Instead of diamonds, spades, clubs, and hearts, they chose "love" symbolized by a flame, "dreams" symbolized by a black star, "revolution" symbolized by a wheel, and "knowledge" symbolized by a lock.

Each artist picked a card out of a hat and had to draw their own version. They chose famous people from history as the face cards. Sixty-two years after leaving Marseille, Aube Breton donated the original drawings made in their final days at the villa to the Cantini Museum in memory of Varian Fry.

Further Reading

Books

Fry, Varian, *Surrender on Demand*, New York, Random House, 1945

Fry, Varian, *Assignment: Rescue, An Autobiography*, New York, Scholastic Inc., 1968

McClafferty, Carla Killough, *In Defiance of Hitler, The Secret Mission of Varian Fry*, New York, Farrar, Straus, Giroux, 2008

Internet

The United States Holocaust Memorial Museum opened with an exhibition on Varian Fry and the Rescue Committee. Their website contains a wealth of material.
http://www.ushmm.org/wlc/en/article.php?ModuleId=10005740

This website is dedicated to the memory of Varian Fry and has links to many other resources.
http://www.almondseed.com/vfry/

The International Rescue Committee, which continues the work that Varian and Danny and so many others did for refugees, works to help refugees around the world today. Their website contains information about Varian Fry as well as what you can do today to help the plight of refuges.
http://www.rescue.org/varian-fry

Yad Vashem, located in Jerusalem, Israel documents the history of the Jews during the Holocaust. Part of their program is called the Righteous Among Nations, which recognizes those individuals who acted with courage and bravery to help save lives. Varian was the first US citizen to be given this honor.
http://www.yadvashem.org/yv/en/righteous/stories/fry.asp

About My Uncle Danny Bénédite and Me.

I met my great-uncle Danny a few times, but I knew him more from the stories my father told. After the war, whenever my father was visiting family in France, it was always Danny who provided the most joyous gatherings. One glorious summer, Danny invited my father and all of his cousins to the island of Ischia. My father remembers wonderful meals there that often ended with Danny leading everyone into song, because just like at Villa Air-Bel, Danny loved to sing.

Later, as an adult, I read Danny's book about the war, La Filiere Marseillaise, and I talked with my grandmother. I began to understand how brave Danny was. Sadly, I never asked him about the war. I was too shy.

Now, I live near Marseille and I recently had to take my family to the American consulate there. I was astonished when I saw a huge photo of Danny in the waiting room. Excitedly, I told my children about their brave great-great-uncle, and I realized this was a story that needed to be told to other children.

I dedicate this to the memory of my grandmother,
Zabeth Bénédite Ungemach Davidson (1914-1996)

Author's note: This is a work of creative nonfiction, based on a true story.
I wish to thank to Aube Breton, Pierre Ungemach, Pierre Sauvage, and
Jean-Michel Guiraud for their help, dedication and generosity.

Design and production by Pinafore Press / Janice Shay

Historic photography, pages 23-35: Daniel Bénédite and Varian Fry, 1940 © Collection Pierre Ungemach, droits réservé, courtesy of the Association Fry. / Aube Breton with her father André Breton, 1940 © Centre Pompidou – Mnam – Bibliotèque Kandinsky. / Aube's mother, Jacqueline Lamba © Collection Aube Breton, courtesy of the Varian Fry Institute. / Aube and her family escape on aboard the ship Capitainne LeMerle, United States Holocaust Memorial Museum Photo Archives #34443, coursety of Dyno Lowenstien Cynthia Jaffee McCabe © United States Holocaust Memorial Museum. / Theo, Peterkin, and Danny on a picnic, circa 1940 © Eva Strauss Paillard./ The Villa Air-Bel where Aube and her family lived in 1940-41 © Varian Fry Institute. / Aube with her mother and father eating breakfast at the Villa Air-Bel, 1940 © Collection Pierre Ungemach, droits réservé, courtesy of the Association Fry. / Sylvain Itkine, Jacques Herold, Aube and her father gathering wood, 1941 © Collection Aube Breton, courtesy of the Varian Fry Institute. / Jacques Herold helping Danny Bénédite in the tree hang the exhibition of Max Ernst, 1940. United States Holocaust Memorial Museum Photo Archives #48833 © United States Holocaust Memorial Museum. / Aube's mother, Jacqueline Lamba, hanging upside down on a swing at the Villa Air-Bel © Collection Aube Breton, courtesy of the Varian Fry Institute.

ISBN: 9781455622658
E-book ISBN: 9781455622665

Printed in China

Published by Pelican Publishing Company, Inc.
1000 Burmaster Street, Gretna, Louisiana 70053